100 Prof
For Power Prom

100 Profits+Plus Ideas
For Power Promoting Your Retail Business

What they say about Tom Shay's Profits+Plus Ideas:

"Retailing is not an easy business to be in these days. Being an independent retailer is even more difficult. With Tom Shay's books and programs, the task is made a lot simpler and success a lot more attainable. With simplified techniques and practical insights on what it takes to satisfy your customers profitably, Tom provides the tools for what every retailer needs to compete in today's marketplace."

Ken Banks, former VP of marketing at *Eckerd Drugs* and *Circuit City*

"Tom addresses topics that are of immediate and urgent concern to retailers."

Marcia Ford, editor of *Christian Retailing*

100 Profits+Plus Ideas
For Power Promoting Your Retail Business

Tom Shay
Copyright © MCMXCVII

All rights reserved.
No part of this book may be used or reproduced
whatsoever without the written permission of the author.
Library of Congress Number: 98-090032
ISBN: 1-891964-01-1

If you enjoyed this book, you'll appreciate the entire series
of Profits+Plus Ideas™ books. These, plus our EZ Cashflow™
software program for independent retailers can be
ordered direct from Profits+Plus Seminars.

☐ 100 ideas for Power Managing ($11.00 including postage)

☐ 100 *more* ideas for Power Promoting ($11.00 including postage)

☐ 100 *new* ideas for Power Managing ($11.00 including postage)

☐ EZ Cashflow™ * ($30.00 including postage)

Send your check and shipping instructions to:

Profits+Plus Seminars
PO Box 1577
St. Petersburg, Fl   33731

* Software requires Microsoft Excel

100 Profits+Plus Ideas

For Power Promoting Your Retail Business

Want a free book?

There are more 100 Profits+Plus books on the way,
and more great ideas where these came from:
retailers just like you!
Submit an idea that is used in the next book,
and we will send you a complimentary copy.

Profits+Plus Seminars
PO Box 1577
St. Petersburg, Fl   33731

100 Profits+Plus Ideas

For Power Promoting Your Retail Business

100 Profits+Plus Ideas is a trademark of Profits+Plus Seminars and Tom Shay, denoting a series of products that may include, but are not limited to:

- Books
- Magazine Articles
- Audio Cassettes
- Video Tapes
- Seminars

Published by:
Profits+Plus Seminars
PO Box 1577
St. Petersburg, Fl 33731

100 Profits+Plus Ideas

For Power Promoting Your Retail Business

The author gives his thanks to:
Karen Saltz, for her teachings
Dennis Chappell, for his encouragement
Jack Rice, for his direction
Marilyn Shay, for her understanding and patience
Shirley and Frank Shay, for their retail education
Larry Winget, for saying, "It's ok"
D. Wendal Attig, for his coaching,
and a special remembrance of
Grandpa Buster Brown, greeting every customer
with, "Hi Neighbor"

100 Profits+Plus Ideas
For Power Promoting Your Retail Business

1.

Keep your store looking fresh

Place a rack or table of merchandise just inside the door. Change the selection every three days.
Display merchandise that is:

- *On sale*
- *Seasonal*
- *New*

Check here if you plan to use this idea ☐

100 Profits+Plus Ideas
For Power Promoting Your Retail Business

2.

Give your customers imprinted items

- If you sell clothing, give them business cards with spare buttons attached.
- If you sell paint, give them painter's caps
- If you sell _____ give them _____

(Brainstorm some ideas with your team)

Check here if you plan to use this idea ☐

100 Profits+Plus Ideas
For Power Promoting Your Retail Business

3.

Make customers see all of your business

Place copies of your advertising in the front
of your business. Display the actual items in
the rear of the department.

Check here if you plan to use this idea ☐

100 Profits+Plus Ideas
For Power Promoting Your Retail Business

4.

Give customers a unique welcome
Most businesses use, "Can I help you?"
Have your employees greet each
customer with a warm hello
and engage them in a conversation.

Check here if you plan to use this idea ☐

100 Profits+Plus Ideas

For Power Promoting Your Retail Business

5.

Optimize your billboard advertising

Billboards should have no more
than seven words on them.

Check here if you plan to use this idea ☐

100 Profits+Plus Ideas
For Power Promoting Your Retail Business

6.

Maximum customer service

Provide a friendly face, and
customer service better than anyone else.
Then, tell your customers about it.

'A friendly greeting at the door,
and all throughout the store.'

Check here if you plan to use this idea ☐

100 Profits+Plus Ideas
For Power Promoting Your Retail Business

7.

Utilize your knowledge

Many local clubs, Rotary, Kiwanis, and Optimists,
are always looking for speakers. This is a
wonderful opportunity to tell the community about
products and services you sell.
If you need to polish your speaking skills,
join a Toastmaster's Club.

Check here if you plan to use this idea ☐

100 Profits+Plus Ideas
For Power Promoting Your Retail Business

8.

End caps sell merchandise
End cap displays should grab the
customer's attention and sell merchandise.
An end cap should sell as much
merchandise as 50 percent of
one side of the adjoining counter.

Check here if you plan to use this idea ☐

100 Profits+Plus Ideas
For Power Promoting Your Retail Business

9.

Be a community involved business

- *Hold a community sidewalk sale*
- *Sponsor your sports teams*
- *Have a float in the town parade*
- *Help the scout troop earn a merit badge*
- *Support the community high school*

Check here if you plan to use this idea ☐

100 Profits+Plus Ideas
For Power Promoting Your Retail Business

10.

Bonus money

Give your employees bonus money for selling:

- *New products*
- *Discontinued items*
- *Higher quality items*
- *Special orders*

Check here if you plan to use this idea ☐

100 Profits+Plus Ideas
For Power Promoting Your Retail Business

11.

Write your customers a letter

Send a letter each month telling your customers
about your employees and the events going on in your store.
Build a mailing list through the names and addresses on:

- *Checks*
- *Service Tickets*
- *Lists from Homeowner Associations*

Check here if you plan to use this idea ☐

100 Profits+Plus Ideas
For Power Promoting Your Retail Business

12.

Utilize coupons in your parking lot

Create "today only" coupons to be placed on the windshields of cars in your parking lot.
Split the cost of the coupons by having another merchant print his coupon on the reverse side.

Check here if you plan to use this idea ☐

100 Profits+Plus Ideas
For Power Promoting Your Retail Business

13.

Give your customers something extra

Every customer, as they leave your store should
be given something to take with them:

- *A copy of your latest sale circular*
- *A photo copy of your newspaper ad*
- *A card listing your services*
- *A coupon*

Check here if you plan to use this idea ☐

100 Profits+Plus Ideas

For Power Promoting Your Retail Business

14.

Participate in "Teach In" Day

Many school systems observe
"teach in" day in November.
Volunteer to teach students about your business.

Check here if you plan to use this idea ☐

100 Profits+Plus Ideas

For Power Promoting Your Retail Business

15.

Maximize your register receipt

Change your register receipt imprint frequently to tell customers about an upcoming event in your business.

Check here if you plan to use this idea ☐

100 Profits+Plus Ideas
For Power Promoting Your Retail Business

16.

Become a media source

Contact your local news media and
volunteer to be a source of expert information
when the news is applicable to your area of retail.

Check here if you plan to use this idea ☐

100 Profits+Plus Ideas
For Power Promoting Your Retail Business

17.

Send birthday greetings
Utilize the information that you obtain
from the driver's license of a customer.
Send a birthday card and note of appreciation
for their business.

Check here if you plan to use this idea ☐

100 Profits+Plus Ideas
For Power Promoting Your Retail Business

18.

Create humorous apparel

Create a cap or t-shirt with a humorous imprint. Use this as a giveaway for:

- *Open house*
- *Grand opening*
- *Anniversary sale*
- *Door prizes*

Check here if you plan to use this idea ☐

100 Profits+Plus Ideas
For Power Promoting Your Retail Business

19.
Bake cookies for your customers

Baking cookies will bring a pleasant aroma
to your business, and give your customers an
unexpected treat; whether you sell or give away cookies.
Contact:
- *Otis Spunkmeyer Cookies*
  - *1-800-287-0760*

Check here if you plan to use this idea ☐

100 Profits+Plus Ideas
For Power Promoting Your Retail Business

20.

Help customers reach you anytime

Install an answering machine to allow customers to call anytime. Invite them to leave questions and requests so you can contact them during the next business day.

Check here if you plan to use this idea ☐

100 Profits+Plus Ideas
For Power Promoting Your Retail Business

21.

Create a bulletin board brag center

Place a bulletin board near your checkout counter and mount complimentary letters that customers send to your business.

Check here if you plan to use this idea ☐

100 Profits+Plus Ideas

For Power Promoting Your Retail Business

22.

Decorate your store

Give your store the appropriate look of the season,
so that customers always see a store with a fresh and new look.
Try using:

- *Crepe paper for interior decoration*
- *Window painting and displays*
- *Pin on buttons for employees*
- *Vests or jackets for employees*

Check here if you plan to use this idea ☐

100 Profits+Plus Ideas
For Power Promoting Your Retail Business

23.

Maximize your competitor's print ads

Display your competitor's print advertising in
your store by highlighting their price and your price.
Comparative phrases that work include:

- *Their sale price; our everyday price*
- *You save when you shop here*
- *Why travel to save pennies?*

Check here if you plan to use this idea ☐

100 Profits+Plus Ideas

For Power Promoting Your Retail Business

24.

Maximize repeat sales

When selling products that suggest repeat sales,
tag the item with a sticker that denotes:

- *Your business name*
- *Address*
- *Phone number*

Check here if you plan to use this idea ☐

100 Profits+Plus Ideas
For Power Promoting Your Retail Business

25.
The equation of a successful business
Price + quality + information + service = value

Check here if you plan to use this idea ☐

100 Profits+Plus Ideas
For Power Promoting Your Retail Business

26.

Customer Appreciation Days

Have quarterly customer appreciation day.
Make it a day of celebration by including:

- *Coupons for next visit discounts*
- *Departmental specials*
- *Entertainment*
- *Refreshments*

Check here if you plan to use this idea ☐

100 Profits+Plus Ideas

For Power Promoting Your Retail Business

27.

Benefit from your donation advertising

If you advertise in a school yearbook or newspaper,
utilize as a part of your ad, a photo of:

- *A popular teacher*
- *A favorite coach*
- *Cheerleaders*
- *Sports team*

Check here if you plan to use this idea ☐

100 Profits+Plus Ideas

For Power Promoting Your Retail Business

28.

Provide gift certificates as donations

When making a donation to an organization,
give a gift certificate so that the winner
will visit your store.

Check here if you plan to use this idea ☐

100 Profits+Plus Ideas

For Power Promoting Your Retail Business

29.

Advertise in unusual places

Businesses that have customers waiting in their lobbies will often welcome a display from your store. These businesses include:

- *Banks*
- *Insurance agencies*
- *Doctor and lawyer offices*

Check here if you plan to use this idea ☐

100 Profits+Plus Ideas
For Power Promoting Your Retail Business

30.

Obtain free advertising
Locate the talk radio and television shows in your trade area. Offer to become a guest to discuss current customer trends in your field of retail expertise.

Check here if you plan to use this idea ☐

100 Profits+Plus Ideas
For Power Promoting Your Retail Business

31.

Signs, signs, signs

Utilize signs throughout your store to call attention to:

- *New items*
- *Closeouts*
- *Features of products*
- *Special prices*

Check here if you plan to use this idea ☐

100 Profits+Plus Ideas
For Power Promoting Your Retail Business

32.

Use large and small shopping carts
While adults are filling a shopping cart
as they shop in your store, children will often be
allowed to select several items if they too,
have a shopping cart.

Check here if you plan to use this idea ☐

100 Profits+Plus Ideas
For Power Promoting Your Retail Business

33.

Watch your word selection

Be careful of using certain words in your advertising. While they have a positive meaning, they may cause a customer to consider the negative connotation.

Examples include:

- *New look*
- *Improved*
- *Lower Prices*

Check here if you plan to use this idea ☐

100 Profits+Plus Ideas
For Power Promoting Your Retail Business

34.

Brag about your employees

Create a print ad featuring a photo of your entire staff, listing their names and giving their years of service in the industry.

Check here if you plan to use this idea ☐

100 Profits+Plus Ideas
For Power Promoting Your Retail Business

35.

Do more business with non profit groups
Promote doing business with non profit groups
by giving extended dating and generous discounts
on their purchases.

Check here if you plan to use this idea ☐

100 Profits+Plus Ideas
For Power Promoting Your Retail Business

36.

Be a hero on the road

Equip your delivery vehicle with the necessary items to provide emergency road side service for a disabled vehicle.

Check here if you plan to use this idea ☐

100 Profits+Plus Ideas

For Power Promoting Your Retail Business

37.

Give out more business cards

Create business cards for all of your employees that have contact with customers.

(Employees will hand out more business cards if their photos are on the card)

Check here if you plan to use this idea ☐

100 Profits+Plus Ideas
For Power Promoting Your Retail Business

38.

Ask churches to promote your Sunday hours

Invite attendees to bring their church bulletin into
your business when shopping on a Sunday.
Record the amount of their purchase on their bulletin and
donate 10% of that amount to their church.

Check here if you plan to use this idea ☐

100 Profits+Plus Ideas

For Power Promoting Your Retail Business

39.

Cross advertise

Invite other merchants
to set up a display within your store.
Examples are:

- *Banks promoting home loans*
- *Masseuse with free back rubs*
- *Art galleries*
- *Stores we like* _____

Check here if you plan to use this idea ☐

100 Profits+Plus Ideas
For Power Promoting Your Retail Business

40.

Have a mystery shopper contest
Create a button promoting your store and give to customers on weekdays. Have a mystery shopper in your store on weekends giving prizes to customers that are wearing the promotional button.

Check here if you plan to use this idea ☐

100 Profits+Plus Ideas
For Power Promoting Your Retail Business

41.

Create your own bag stuffers
Make photo copies of your newspaper ads
and use them as bag stuffers.

Check here if you plan to use this idea ☐

100 Profits+Plus Ideas
For Power Promoting Your Retail Business

42.

"Sweet" advertising for the customer

Have a mint or lollipop wrapper imprinted with
the name and address of your business. In addition
to using this as a give away at your checkout counters,
you can find restaurants that would give
your mint or lollipop as an after dinner
reward to their customers.

Check here if you plan to use this idea ☐

100 Profits+Plus Ideas
For Power Promoting Your Retail Business

43.

Charge account reminders

Send statements quarterly to customers that
do not have an outstanding balance.
Include a handwritten note:
*"You owe us nothing, but we wish you did.
Please come to see us soon."*

Check here if you plan to use this idea ☐

100 Profits+Plus Ideas
For Power Promoting Your Retail Business

44.

Create your own food drive

Have a year round policy of offering
a $5 discount on any purchase over $100
if the customer will bring to your store at
least two cans of nonperishable food.

Check here if you plan to use this idea ☐

100 Profits+Plus Ideas

For Power Promoting Your Retail Business

45.

Entertain the kids

Create within your store, a play area designed for kids while their parents are shopping.

Check here if you plan to use this idea ☐

100 Profits+Plus Ideas
For Power Promoting Your Retail Business

46.

Make your business card a keeper
Imprint the back of your business card.
*"I enjoyed doing business with you today,
and know that you would also enjoy
doing business with our organization.
Please come in to see us, bring this card,
and let me know when you arrive."*

Check here if you plan to use this idea ☐

100 Profits+Plus Ideas
For Power Promoting Your Retail Business

47.

Sell those turkeys

Have a turkey sale each year the week preceding Thanksgiving. Use end caps and sale tables to display merchandise at substantially reduced prices.

Check here if you plan to use this idea ☐

100 Profits+Plus Ideas

For Power Promoting Your Retail Business

48.

Have an "olden day" sale

Contact the local antique automobile club and
invite them to have an auto show on your parking lot.
Tie into the event with an
"antique cars & antique prices" sale.

Check here if you plan to use this idea ☐

100 Profits+Plus Ideas
For Power Promoting Your Retail Business

49.

Hats off to everyone

Create a display in your store that is a collection of hats.
Have an imprinted baseball cap made for your store that
you can offer in exchange for hats
that are added to the display.

Check here if you plan to use this idea ☐

100 Profits+Plus Ideas

For Power Promoting Your Retail Business

50.

Promote children's shopping hours

Have a special afternoon for children to shop in your store.
Offer snacks, drinks, and children's entertainment.
Create selections of gifts that are:

- *Less than $5*
- *Less than $10*
- *Less than $20*

Check here if you plan to use this idea ☐

100 Profits+Plus Ideas
For Power Promoting Your Retail Business

51.

Have an after Christmas sale

Provide your customers with a paper grocery sack,
and have a 3 day after Christmas bag sale.
*(Use a large rubber stamp to imprint,
"__% off everything you can put into this bag")*

Check here if you plan to use this idea ☐

100 Profits+Plus Ideas
For Power Promoting Your Retail Business

52.

Support fund raising dinners

When civic groups are having fund raising breakfasts or dinners,
purchase several tickets and use them for
employee incentives or as prizes for contests.

Check here if you plan to use this idea ☐

100 Profits+Plus Ideas
For Power Promoting Your Retail Business

53.

Happy Anniversary!
Even if you do not know the correct date,
have an anniversary sale.

Check here if you plan to use this idea ☐

100 Profits+Plus Ideas
For Power Promoting Your Retail Business

54.

Support the local blood bank

Conduct a blood drive in your parking lot.
Provide the blood bank with
a donor gift and refreshments.

Check here if you plan to use this idea ☐

100 Profits+Plus Ideas
For Power Promoting Your Retail Business

55.

Provide referrals

Create for your customers a list of referrals to other businesses and services. Request feedback regarding the quality of service

Check here if you plan to use this idea ☐

100 Profits+Plus Ideas
For Power Promoting Your Retail Business

56.

Discounts for special orders
Offer a discount to customers when they prepay for a special order.

Check here if you plan to use this idea ☐

100 Profits+Plus Ideas
For Power Promoting Your Retail Business

57.

Here comes the bride

Look for the items in your store
that could be selected for a wedding gift.
Create your own bridal registry, in
addition to locating a traditional bridal store
to exchange referrals with.

Check here if you plan to use this idea ☐

100 Profits+Plus Ideas
For Power Promoting Your Retail Business

58.

Support the local schools
Give away to students
pencils with their school
football or basketball schedule and
your store name and address imprinted on them.

Check here if you plan to use this idea ☐

100 Profits+Plus Ideas
For Power Promoting Your Retail Business

59.

Have a "color sale"

Observe the holidays with a 20% off any item that has any of the particular color on it.

- *Red for Valentine's Day*
- *Green for St. Patrick's Day*
- *Orange for Hulloween*
- *_____ for _____*

(Brainstorm some ideas with your team)

Check here if you plan to use this idea ☐

100 Profits+Plus Ideas
For Power Promoting Your Retail Business

60.

Pay the parking meter

Create 4" x 6" cards with a smiley face
and glue on nickels for the eyes.
*"Parking today is provided with the
compliments and appreciation
of (your business)".*

Check here if you plan to use this idea ☐

100 Profits+Plus Ideas
For Power Promoting Your Retail Business

61.

Community bulletin board

Create a community bulletin board
near your check out counter.
Invite customers to post notice of:

- *Garage Sales*
- *Community events*
- *Neighborhood association meetings*

Check here if you plan to use this idea ☐

100 Profits+Plus Ideas
For Power Promoting Your Retail Business

62.

Use sales representatives

Invite sales representatives that call on your store
to be in your store as a part of a promotion.
The sales representative can:

- *Explain their products*
- *Perform demonstrations*
- *Give out samples*

Check here if you plan to use this idea ☐

100 Profits+Plus Ideas
For Power Promoting Your Retail Business

63.

Promote with the U.S. currency

Stock your cash registers with $2 bills and
Susan B. Anthony dollars.
Customers will think of your store
as these unique currencies change
hands in your community.

Check here if you plan to use this idea ☐

100 Profits+Plus Ideas
For Power Promoting Your Retail Business

64.

Become a bill payment center

Become a collection center for payments of utility bills.

- *Electric*
- *Gas*
- *Telephone*
- *Phone*
- *Water*
- *Sanitation*
- *Cable television*

Check here if you plan to use this idea ☐

100 Profits+Plus Ideas
For Power Promoting Your Retail Business

65.

Offer a photo copy service

Install a 5 cent per copy service in your store. Save money on the cost of your copy machine and make as much as 40% on the service.

Check here if you plan to use this idea ☐

100 Profits+Plus Ideas
For Power Promoting Your Retail Business

66.
Eliminate disclaimers
Make your advertising unique by removing the "small print" and limitations from your advertising.

Check here if you plan to use this idea ☐

100 Profits+Plus Ideas
For Power Promoting Your Retail Business

67.

Appreciate your customers

Have your employees write notes
of appreciation on the statements
you send to customers each month.

Check here if you plan to use this idea ☐

100 Profits+Plus Ideas
For Power Promoting Your Retail Business

68.

Create an employee classroom

Designate a room within your business
as an employee classroom.
Have as a part of the classroom:

- *Table and chairs*
- *Motivational posters*
- *Training material from your vendors*

Check here if you plan to use this idea ☐

100 Profits+Plus Ideas
For Power Promoting Your Retail Business

69.

Give refreshments to your customers

On a cold day, prepare a jug of
hot apple cider and place it with
paper cups near your front entrance.
Invite your customers to help themselves
or utilize a greeter to serve the drink.

Check here If you plan to use this idea ☐

100 Profits+Plus Ideas
For Power Promoting Your Retail Business

70.

Play the name game

Post a sign board near your front entrance, listing a different first name every day. Offer a special discount or a free item to customers with that name.

Check here if you plan to use this idea ☐

100 Profits+Plus Ideas
For Power Promoting Your Retail Business

71.

Use "here's a hint" cards

Place cards on counters about your business that are a folded 3"x5", with your store logo on the cover, and this imprint inside:

"When I was shopping (your store) I saw _____ which I would really enjoy owning. The person that was waiting on me was _____ and the phone number at (your store) is _____."

Check here if you plan to use this idea ☐

100 Profits+Plus Ideas

For Power Promoting Your Retail Business

72.

Intentionally lose money

Have an event or promotion designed to lose money. Make a point to show customers that you value them more than money.
You can:

- *Have several items for sale at a noticeably below cost price*
- *Support a charitable group with no expectation of reimbursement*

Check here if you plan to use this idea ☐

100 Profits+Plus Ideas
For Power Promoting Your Retail Business

73.

Create a drop off center

Become a drop off center for repairs or other services that allow you to be a convenient place for customers. You can offer:

- *Alterations*
- *Lamp repair*
- *Vacuum cleaner repair*
- *Scissors sharpening*

Check here if you plan to use this idea ☐

100 Profits+Plus Ideas

For Power Promoting Your Retail Business

74.

Review your direct mail procedure

Send your sales circulars in more than one mailing to see where you get the best response.

You can categorize your mailings according to:

- *Rural vs. city*
- *East vs. west*
- *Mailing list vs. charge customers*

Check here if you plan to use this idea ☐

100 Profits+Plus Ideas
For Power Promoting Your Retail Business

75.

Saving bags as a cause

Support environmental efforts by offering a 50 cent rebate when customers bring in their own bags to carry home their purchases.

Check here if you plan to use this idea ☐

100 Profits+Plus Ideas
For Power Promoting Your Retail Business

76.

Promote New Year's resolutions

Have a contest asking customers for their
New Year's resolutions. Award prizes according to:

- *Most unusual*
- *Most sincere*
- *Most conservative*
- *Most _____*
  (Brainstorm with your team)

Check here if you plan to use this idea ☐

100 Profits+Plus Ideas

For Power Promoting Your Retail Business

77.

Support Christmas tree lot sales

Invite a charitable group to sell Christmas trees on your parking lot. You can assist with:

- *Cash register*
- *Paper and plastic bags*
- *Promotion in your advertising*

Check here if you plan to use this idea ☐

100 Profits+Plus Ideas
For Power Promoting Your Retail Business

78.

Hold an evening preview sale

Close your store early on the evening before a major sale and invite customers on your mailing list to an "invitation only" sale.

Add:
- *Refreshments*
- *Entertainment*
- *Door prizes*

Check here if you plan to use this idea ☐

100 Profits+Plus Ideas
For Power Promoting Your Retail Business

79.

Have contests during sales

Have drawings for special items during every sale you have. Announce the winners via a poster displayed in your store.

Check here if you plan to use this idea ☐

100 Profits+Plus Ideas
For Power Promoting Your Retail Business

80.

Hold a "Dutch auction"

Get rid of old merchandise using
a "Dutch auction". Place all of the sale
merchandise on one counter with a sign indicating:
- *10% off regular price during 1st week*
- *20% off regular price during 2nd week*
- *30% off regular price during 3rd week*
- *40% off regular price during 4th week*

Check here if you plan to use this idea ☐

100 Profits+Plus Ideas
For Power Promoting Your Retail Business

81.

Create a birthday sale

Offer to customers a 25% discount on anything in the store when they present proper identification on their birthday.

Check here if you plan to use this idea ☐

100 Profits+Plus Ideas
For Power Promoting Your Retail Business

82.

Make a list of gift ideas

Print a bag stuffer that is a list of "101 great gift ideas from (your store)."
Change the list for:

- *Birthday gifts*
- *Christmas gifts*
- *Anniversary gifts*
- *Special occasion gifts*

Check here if you plan to use this idea ☐

100 Profits+Plus Ideas
For Power Promoting Your Retail Business

83.

Display your print advertising
Place copies of your
newspaper ads and direct mail
pieces throughout your store
for your customers to see.

Check here if you plan to use this idea ☐

100 Profits+Plus Ideas
For Power Promoting Your Retail Business

84.

Participate in home shows

Check with the Chamber of Commerce
to sign up for the home show in the local
convention center. Rent a space
to display your goods and services.
Be sure to give away imprinted items.

Check here if you plan to use this idea ☐

100 Profits+Plus Ideas
For Power Promoting Your Retail Business

85.

Have a "name your charity" sale

Create a list of charities in your community
and allow customers to designate
10% of their purchase to be
given to the local charity.

Check here if you plan to use this idea ☐

100 Profits+Plus Ideas
For Power Promoting Your Retail Business

86.

Donate your classroom

Invite civic groups and neighborhood associations to use your classroom for their meetings. Be sure to have copies of your advertising displayed in the room.

Check here if you plan to use this idea ☐

100 Profits+Plus Ideas
For Power Promoting Your Retail Business

87.

Have a "blind auction"

Select a product each month for
a "blind auction". Invite customers to
submit their bids written on an entry
form with all proceeds being given to the school.

Check here if you plan to use this idea ☐

100 Profits+Plus Ideas

For Power Promoting Your Retail Business

88.

Maximize your postage

Your first class postage stamp entitles
you to an envelope weighing one ounce.
Get your money's worth and
fill your monthly statements with
information about products or services you sell.

Check here if you plan to use this idea ☐

100 Profits+Plus Ideas
For Power Promoting Your Retail Business

89.

Promote with soft drink vendors

Many soft drink vendors have a concession food wagon offering a hot dog and a fountain vended drink for $1.00. Your cost is usually 50 cents. Use a civic group to staff the wagon during a promotion and donate 100% of the food wagon proceeds to their group.

Check here if you plan to use this idea ☐

100 Profits+Plus Ideas
For Power Promoting Your Retail Business

90.
Offer gift wrapping

Find a unique gift wrap paper that is suitable for year round usage. During major shopping seasons have a civic group offer free gift wrapping in your store. You supply the gift wrap, tape, and accessories. The civic group keeps all of the donations.

Check here if you plan to use this idea ☐

100 Profits+Plus Ideas
For Power Promoting Your Retail Business

91.

Have a Santa Claus service

Invite children to send their "Dear Santa"
letters to Santa in care of your store.
Parents are then invited to come
to your store to see your special
"Santa postal station" and pick up
the letter their child wrote.

Check here if you plan to use this idea ☐

100 Profits+Plus Ideas
For Power Promoting Your Retail Business

92.

Create a "Wall of Fame"

When customers, or their businesses, have an article written about them in a magazine or newspaper, frame the article and hang it in your store.

Check here if you plan to use this idea ☐

100 Profits+Plus Ideas
For Power Promoting Your Retail Business

93.

Have a Christmas tree auction

Display four artificial Christmas trees, and
invite four civic groups to bring their ornaments
to decorate the tree. Have a "blind auction"
for each of the decorated trees, with
all of the proceeds going to the respective groups.

Check here if you plan to use this idea ☐

100 Profits+Plus Ideas
For Power Promoting Your Retail Business

94.

Give away fresh popcorn

Using plain white paper bags, and
a rubber stamp with your store imprint,
you can pop corn and have your
customers enjoy it while they shop
in your store.

Check here if you plan to use this idea ☐

100 Profits+Plus Ideas
For Power Promoting Your Retail Business

95.

Have "how to clinics"

Whatever you sell or service, customers appreciate the opportunity to learn more about their options as they shop. Offer 30 to 60 minute classes taught by your employees.

Check here if you plan to use this idea ☐

100 Profits+Plus Ideas
For Power Promoting Your Retail Business

96.

Give rain check discounts

When you have to issue a rain check, offer the customer a 10% discount for the inconvenience of having to return to complete their purchase.

Check here if you plan to use this idea ☐

100 Profits+Plus Ideas
For Power Promoting Your Retail Business

97.

Have a "name your own sale" sale

Print a coupon entitling
a customer to 25% off any
one item of their choice.

Check here if you plan to use this idea ☐

100 Profits+Plus Ideas

For Power Promoting Your Retail Business

98.

Give away "Santa key chains"

Purchase a plastic key fob that has your store imprint on one side and "House key for Santa" on the other. Place miscut keys that you obtain from a hardware store on the key ring, to give to parents, grandparents, and children as they shop in your store.

Check here if you plan to use this idea ☐

100 Profits+Plus Ideas
For Power Promoting Your Retail Business

99.

Locate co-op advertising dollars

Manufacturers and wholesalers often have available co-op dollars which will reimburse you for part or all of your advertising expenses.

Check here if you plan to use this idea ☐

100 Profits+Plus Ideas
For Power Promoting Your Retail Business

100.

Anyone can advertise but it takes a PRO to PROMOTE!

Check here if you plan to use this idea ☐